NICKI MINAJ

TWO EXTRAORDINARY PEOPLE.

CARDI B

CONNECTED LIVES™

Ariana Grande | Camila Cabello

Ed Sheeran | Shawn Mendes

Halsey | Billie Eilish

John Legend | Michael Bublé

Kacey Musgraves | Maren Morris

Kane Brown | Sam Hunt

Kendrick Lamar | Travis Scott

Nicki Minaj | Cardi B

Photo credits: page 4: Leon Bennett via Getty Images; page 5: Ethan Miller via Getty Images; page 9: Dimitrios Kambouris / Diamond Ball via Getty Images; page 10: Alexander Spatari / Moment via Getty Images; page 11: Fernelis Lajara / EyeEm via Getty Images; page 12: Dimitrios Kambouris / Elizabeth Arden via Getty Images; page 13: Scott Legato / Live Nation via Getty Images; page 16: Kevin Winter via Getty Images; page 17: Matt Winkelmeyer via Getty Images; page 18: Frazer Harrison via Getty Images; page 19: Rachel Murray / REVOLVE via Getty Images; page 20: Bryan Bedder via Getty Images; page 21: littleny / iStock Editorial via Getty Images; page 22: Larry Busacca / TIDAL via Getty Images; page 23: Frederick M. Brown via Getty Images; page 24: Kevin Winter via Getty Images; page 28: Christopher Polk / A+E Networks via Getty Images; page 29: Jamie McCarthy via Getty Images; page 30: Ethan Miller via Getty Images; page 31: Ethan Miller / iHeartMedia via Getty Images; page 32: Larry Busacca / Pepsi via Getty Images; page 33: Scott Legato / Live Nation via Getty Images; page 34: Larry Busacca / Pepsi via Getty Images; page 37: Gustavo Caballero / BET via Getty Images; page 40: Kevin Winter via Getty Images; page 41: Rich Polk / iHeartMedia via Getty Images; page 42: Larry Busacca / Pepsi via Getty Images; page 45: Joe Scarnici / Pandora Media Inc. via Getty Images; page 46: Christopher Polk / MTV via Getty Images; page 47: Amy Sussman via Getty Images; page 48: Kevin Winter via Getty Images; page 49: Theo Wargo via Getty Images; page 52: Jason Merritt via Getty Images; page 53: Christopher Polk via Getty Images; page 54: David Becker via Getty Images; page 56: Michael Buckner / Clear Channel via Getty Images; page 57: David Becker via Getty Images; page 58: Ethan Miller / iHeartMedia via Getty Images; page 62: Kevin Winter via Getty Images; page 63: Kevin Winter / NARAS via Getty Images; page 64: Stephen Lovekin / Bud Light via Getty Images, Ethan Miller via Getty Images; background: Chris Wong / EyeEm via Getty Images; Cardi B head shot: Mike Coppola / TIDAL via Getty Images; Nicki Minaj head shot: Bryan Bedder via Getty Images

ISBN: 978-1-68021-794-0
eBook: 978-1-64598-080-3

Printed in Malaysia

24 23 22 21 20   1 2 3 4 5

TABLE OF CONTENTS

CHAPTER 1

EARLY LIFE

WHO IS NICKI MINAJ?

Rapper Nicki Minaj was born on December 8, 1982. Before she was known as Nicki, she was Onika Tanya Maraj. Her family lived in Saint James. This is a district of Port of Spain, the capital city of Trinidad and Tobago. The Caribbean country is made up of two main islands. They sit seven miles off the coast of South America.

WHO IS CARDI B?

Belcalis Marlenis Almanzar was born almost ten years after Nicki, on October 11, 1992. People know her as the rapper Cardi B. Her parents lived in the Bronx. This is a borough in New York City. It is north of Manhattan, where her grandmother lived. Cardi B spent a lot of time at her grandmother's home in the neighborhood of Washington Heights.

A LARGE FAMILY

Nicki's parents are Robert and Carol. Her dad is of Indo-Trinidadian descent. This means he has African and Indian heritage. Carol is of Afro-Trinidadian descent. Nicki is one-quarter Indian. In Trinidad, Carol was an accounting clerk. Later in life, she became a gospel singer. Robert worked at American Express when they moved to the United States. The family has four children. Jelani is Nicki's older brother. Micaiah and Ming are her younger brother and sister.

Port of Spain, Trinidad and Tobago

THE OLDEST SISTER

Like Nicki's, Cardi B's parents have a Caribbean background. Her mother is also from Trinidad and Tobago. Carlos, her dad, comes from the Dominican Republic. He worked as a taxi driver. Her mom was a cashier. Cardi B's family is smaller than Nicki's. She has one younger sister named Hennessy Carolina. The sisters have six younger half-siblings too. However, they didn't grow up with Cardi B.

MUSIC IN TRINIDAD AND TOBAGO

Several types of music began in Trinidad and Tobago. It is the home of calypso music. This has influences from western Africa and South America. Steel pan drums were also first used in Trinidad and Tobago. One big tradition that involves music is Carnival. The huge festival happens every year. People wear elaborate costumes. They dance and sing in the streets.

Saint James, Trinidad and Tobago

SAINT JAMES

When Nicki was three years old, her parents
moved from Trinidad and Tobago to New York
City. The couple wanted to provide a better life to their
children. There were more opportunities in the United
States. They attended school and looked for work. Nicki
stayed in Saint James with her grandmother. "I thought
it was going to be for a few days, it turned into two years
without my mother," she said on MTV.

WASHINGTON HEIGHTS

Cardi B's grandmother lived in an apartment in Washington Heights. Her home was small. It was always full of people though. The singer's aunts or some of her 36 cousins might be there at any time. As a kid, she spent a lot of time at the apartment. Even as an adult, it is one of her favorite spots. She told *Vibe* it's still her "happy place."

CARIBBEAN MUSICIANS

Many famous musicians are from the Caribbean. Some are from the island of Jamaica, like the rapper Shaggy. Heavy D and Bob Marley were also from there. Marley was one of the first reggae singers in the United States. Sean Paul is a Jamaican reggae singer too.

Barbados is another Caribbean island. One of the first hip-hop DJs, Grandmaster Flash, grew up there. The singer Rihanna is also from Barbados.

Rihanna

MOVING TO THE BIG CITY

Nicki was five years old when she moved to New York. Her parents had found a place to live in Queens. "A lot of times when you're from the islands, your parents leave and then send for you," she said on MTV. That's what her parents did. The future star was excited to move to New York. She said, "I thought it was gonna be like a castle." Her first memory was of how cold it was. "I had never seen snow," she remembered.

"GIRL FROM THE BRONX"

Cardi B spent her childhood in New York. "I am just a girl from the Bronx," she told the *New York Post*. The Bronx is not far from where Nicki grew up in Queens. Cardi B's family lived in the Highbridge neighborhood. Most of the residents there are Latino. The rapper grew up speaking Spanish. That was her first language.

Bronx, New York City

DIFFICULT CHILDHOOD

Nicki went through some rough years during her
childhood. Her father struggled with drug abuse. He
was violent toward her mother. Eventually, he got
help. Still, those early years were hard on his daughter.
She invented different personalities. These helped her
cope. "I would imagine being a new person," Nicki told
New York magazine. One of her earliest characters was
Harajuku Barbie. This character was obsessed with the
color pink.

BULLIED IN SCHOOL

Middle school was hard for Cardi B. She started sixth grade at a new school. Her classmates made fun of her clothes. Cardi B wore bright pink skirts. Jackets with fake fur on them grabbed attention. Students bullied her for being different. Around the same time, her parents got divorced.

DREAMS OF SUCCESS

As a child, Nicki saw her mother struggle. Her father could not hold down a job. His addiction made him unstable. Her mom worked hard to keep the family going. Seeing this gave Nicki a goal in life. Succeeding would let her take care of her mom. Nicki knew it was up to her to make it happen. "My mom motivated me, but it wasn't a strict household," she said on the TV show *The View*.

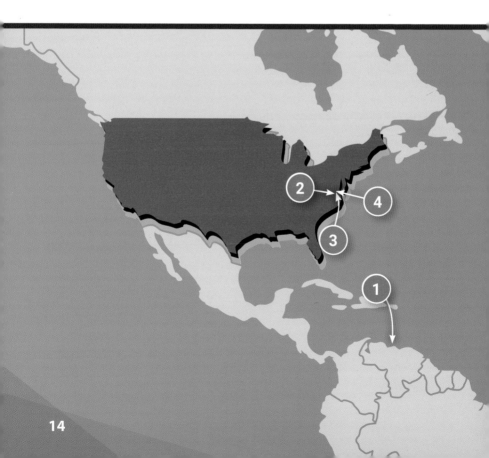

STRICT PARENTS

As a child, Cardi B suffered from severe asthma. Sometimes she would have to stay in the hospital. Her stays could last two weeks. This worried her mom and dad. They wanted to protect her. She told *Dazed*, "I had very strict parents, I could never go outside or go to parties." This was the opposite of Nicki's home life.

NICKI MINAJ

1. **Saint James, Trinidad and Tobago:** This is where Nicki was born. She lived here with her grandmother until she was five.

2. **Queens, New York:** After moving here when she was five, this is where Nicki spent her childhood.

CARDI B

3. **Washington Heights, Manhattan:** Cardi B's grandmother lives here. This where Cardi B spent much of her childhood.

4. **The Bronx, New York:** This is where Cardi B's family moved when she was in the sixth grade.

CHAPTER 2

INTRO TO MUSIC

NATURAL PERFORMER

From a young age, Nicki liked to perform. "Everywhere we went, I was up singing or acting," she told *New York* magazine. Nicki's love of entertaining formed naturally while growing up. In school, she played the clarinet. Choir gave her a place to sing. By the time Nicki was 12, she had written her first rap song. The next step was to audition for a performing arts high school. She hoped to attend Fiorello H. LaGuardia High School of Music & Art and Performing Arts.

LEARNING TO BE A STAR

Like Nicki, Cardi B had grown up singing at home. "My grandmother always used to make me sing for her," she explained to MTV News. "You're going to be such a star," her grandmother told her. That encouragement led the teenager to attend Renaissance High School for Musical Theater and the Arts. The school was in the Bronx. It was similar to where Nicki wanted to go. Both schools taught students how to perform. Some were singers. Others wanted to be actors.

LAGUARDIA HIGH SCHOOL

Unfortunately, LaGuardia High School had bad news for Nicki. They turned her down as a singer. However, they would let her study acting. Acting was an important part of high school for both women. Nicki already had informal experience. Her different characters were a kind of acting. Sometimes she used a British or Jamaican accent for them. This had prepared her for taking on different roles in high school.

PERFORMING ARTS HIGH SCHOOLS

Nicki and Cardi B both went to high schools that prepared teenagers for the performing arts. Students usually have to audition to get into these. Spots are limited. Many famous singers, musicians, and actors have come out of these schools. Timothée Chalamet, Awkwafina, and Ansel Elgort all studied at the same school as Nicki.

Awkwafina

A ROCKY START

Cardi B sang Madonna's "Material Girl" in her freshman talent show. As a high school senior, she sang Lady Gaga's "Bad Romance." She loved to perform. School wasn't always her top priority though. Having fun with friends was important to her. Cardi B earned roles in several musicals. Then she lost them. Her grades were too low. The rapper later told students at her high school that teachers kept telling her, "Why are you not taking these things seriously? You're so smart!"

WAITING FOR A CHANCE

Nicki loved school. "I majored in drama and theater. We had all the freedom in the world to do any and everything we wanted," she told *Wonderland* magazine. Still, Nicki ran into obstacles after graduation. New York was full of people who wanted to act. It was hard for her to break into the acting scene. She took a job as a waitress at Red Lobster.

Borough of Manhattan
Community College

FINDING HER PATH

In high school, Cardi B's personality shone
through, even offstage. She graduated in
2010. Classmates voted her Most Dramatic in the school
yearbook. Her next step was enrolling in the Borough of
Manhattan Community College. There, she took French
and history classes. After three semesters, she decided
college wasn't the right path for her.

WORK INSPIRATION

Nicki thought up rap lyrics while working. "I would take people's order and then a rap might come to me just by what they're wearing or what they said or did," she remarked to the *New York Times*. "I would go in the kitchen and write it down. . . . By the time I was done, I would have all of these sheets of paper thrown around everywhere with raps," she added.

A NEW JOB

After high school, Cardi B worked part-time as a cashier at an Amish market. The store fired her for giving discounts to friends. Her boss suggested she look for work across the street as an exotic dancer. At age 19, she decided to give it a try. It wasn't going to be a long-term job. Cardi B told herself she'd quit by age 25. This gave her a limit. Around this same time, she started posting videos on Instagram and Vine. There was no singing or rapping in them. Instead, the videos were observations about life.

BACKUP SINGER

Nicki's job as a waitress didn't last very long. She wasn't always polite to customers. In about five years, she was fired from 15 jobs. Finally, Nicki found work as a backup singer. Rappers in New York hired her. One job was for Full Force. This was a group of rap and hip-hop artists and producers. The singer recorded backup music on several of their tracks.

SOCIAL MEDIA

While Nicki was writing lyrics during her day job, Cardi B was trying to build a social media following. People thought she was funny. They also appreciated how honest she was. Many of her videos went viral. It didn't take long for her to gain over 100,000 followers on Instagram.

Cardi B had a secret goal. Sometimes she thought about a music career. "I was always scared to follow my dreams because if I follow my dreams and I fail, I can't dream about it anymore," she told *The Fader*.

REALITY TV STARS

Many musicians have been discovered on reality shows. Even if the contestants didn't win, they developed a fan base. Usher and Christina Aguilera both appeared on *Star Search*. Neither artist won. *American Idol* is another show that has launched many careers. Kelly Clarkson and Carrie Underwood both won their seasons. Adam Lambert didn't win his, but he still became very popular.

HOOD$TARS

Some members of Full Force created a new group in the early 2000s. It was called Hood$tars. Nicki was the only female rapper in the quartet. The other members were Lou$tar, Scaff Beezy, and 7even Up. Nicki didn't stay with the group for very long. Soon, she began posting more and more of her rap videos online.

LOVE AND HIP-HOP

While Nicki's career was taking a traditional path, Cardi B headed in a different direction. She became famous on social media first. The music career came later. Television producers noticed that many people followed her on social media. They invited her to be on a reality show. Cardi B was cast on season six of *Love & Hip Hop: New York (LHHNY)*. The show follows artists and producers. It also documents people who want to make it in the industry.

PARALLEL LIVES

Born in Saint James, Trinidad and Tobago

Has two brothers and one sister

Performs under a stage name

Family from Trinidad and Tobago

Discovered on social media

Born in Washington Heights, Manhattan

Has one sister and six half-siblings

Bullied in school

CHAPTER 3

RISE TO SUCCESS

MYSPACE

Nicki had been posting songs to her MySpace page for a few years. She also sent them to people in the music industry. Getting noticed wasn't easy. "My journey to who I am today began on MySpace," she told *Teen Vogue*. Rapper and producer Fendi found Nicki's music online in 2006. He signed her to his record label, Dirty Money. Her first contract was only for 180 days. This was the break she needed.

GETTING SERIOUS

Cardi B was cast again for season seven of *LHHNY*.
Then, in 2016, she announced she would be leaving to
work on music. Her new manager noticed something.
She had been rewriting lyrics to songs from popular
artists, like Beyoncé. Cardi B was putting her own spin
on them. He encouraged her to
continue. The manager thought
she had the potential to become
a star.

LIL WAYNE

Fendi introduced Nicki to someone who would take her career even further. This was rapper Lil Wayne. "I give Wayne credit because he saw me and pretty much picked me out of a lineup," she told *The Fader*. The big star helped Nicki put together three mixtapes between 2007 and 2009. These helped her reach a bigger audience. *Billboard* named her an "artist to watch" in 2010.

Lil Wayne

Shaggy

MAKING MIXTAPES

Cardi B had already been featured on Shaggy's remix of "Boom Boom" in 2015. She ended up releasing a single a month later. Then the rapper made two hip-hop mixtapes in 2016 and 2017. As they were for Nicki, mixtapes were Cardi B's next big step in building her music career.

YOUNG MONEY

By 2009, Lil Wayne had signed Nicki onto his record label. It is called Young Money. Later that year, she performed on his album *We Are Young Money*. Many artists were on the record, including Drake. Nicki also started working on recording her debut studio album. "This is my time, and it makes me feel like I need to deliver a classic album. I don't want to let people down that get excited about me," she told *Billboard*.

Lil Wayne

ATLANTIC RECORDS

Cardi B's popularity couldn't be ignored. The mixtapes
she released did well. More than 6 million people
followed her on Instagram. Atlantic Records signed
her in 2017. The rapper had wanted to keep working as
an independent artist. However, the label offered her
a good contract. "I felt like it's certain things that are
harder when you're an independent artist, like get on
the radio, go to certain shows, be considered serious,"
she told *The Fader*.

"MASSIVE ATTACK"

The track "Massive Attack" was supposed to be on Nicki's first album. It would be the lead single. This is a song released before an album comes out. A lead single gets audiences excited about the music. However, the song didn't do as well as Nicki and her producers had hoped. "Massive Attack" didn't even make it onto the Hot 100 list. It was dropped from the album.

"BODAK YELLOW"

Cardi B's lead single for her first studio album got the opposite reaction. While Nicki's had flopped, the Bronx singer's became a huge success. "Bodak Yellow" came out in 2017. It worked its way up the chart until it hit number one. By 2019, it had gone nine times platinum. This was a big deal for Cardi B's career. She became the second female solo rapper to have a song reach number one. Lauryn Hill had been the first in 1998.

GOING PLATINUM

The Recording Industry Association of America keeps track of how many albums and singles sell. This is one way of showing how popular music is. There are three categories of high sales: gold, platinum, and diamond. A gold record is an album that has sold 500,000 copies. Platinum is for 1 million. Diamond records have sold over 10 million copies.

"Bodak Yellow" went nine times platinum. More than 9 million copies were sold in the U.S. as of September 2019.

BEST NEW ARTIST

Despite a few setbacks, Nicki's career was taking off. "Your Love" was released as the new lead single for her album. The song came out in June 2010. It was much more popular than "Massive Attack." Later that month, the artist won her first and second Black Entertainment Television (BET) Awards. She won Best New Artist and Best Female Hip-Hop Artist. Her first studio album hadn't even been released yet.

FRIENDS OR FEUD?

In 2017, "No Flags" came out. Nicki rapped the line "I heard these labels tryna make another me." People thought it was meant as an insult to Cardi B. Later that year, the two artists collaborated with the rap group Migos on "MotorSport." Fans thought that their verses sounded like a rap fight.

The two denied the feud. Still, rumors continued. Then they got into a fight at New York Fashion Week in September 2018. Cardi B had felt insulted by some of Nicki's online posts.

VIEWERS' CHOICE

Cardi B was slowly getting more recognition too. In 2017, she had been nominated for two BET Awards. She didn't win, though. That changed the next year. "Bodak Yellow" got a viewers' choice award at the BETs. That year, Cardi B also won the same award that Nicki had won eight years earlier. It was for Best Female Hip-Hop Artist.

FEELING NERVOUS

Many people liked Nicki's rapping. But she wasn't sure if wider audiences would like her. When her music started to get more popular, she didn't know how people would react. "At the beginning, I was very nervous," she said to *The Fader*. By fall of 2010, she was setting records. That year, she was the first female rapper to ever sing at Yankee Stadium. Seven of her songs were on the Hot 100 list. This was a new record for a female solo artist.

INSECURITIES

In 2017, Cardi B's popularity was growing. No other person of Dominican descent had made it to the top of the Hot 100 list before. She hadn't even released a major studio album yet. Still, the rapper had some doubts. "Bartier Cardi" came out in late 2017. The song was a hit. It had taken a while to record it though. Cardi B redid the song multiple times until she felt like it was right. This happened with many of her songs. She explained to *GQ*, "I'm really insecure about my accent when it comes to music. In person, I don't care."

CAREER MILESTONES

2010

Nicki's debut studio album *Pink Friday* is released.

2011

Nicki wins two American Music Awards (AMAs) for Favorite Rap/Hip-Hop Album and Favorite Artist Rap/Hip-Hop.

2015

Cardi B is featured on Shaggy's remix of "Boom Boom." This is her first recording.

2017

Nicki claims the Guinness World Record for most Billboard Hot 100 entries by a solo artist (female).

2017

Cardi B releases hit song "Bodak Yellow." It reaches number one on the charts.

2018

Nicki releases the album *Queen*.

2018

Cardi B sets Guinness World Record for most simultaneous Billboard U.S. Hot 100 entries by a female. She also wins an AMA for Favorite Artist Rap/Hip-Hop.

2019

Nicki's single and music video "Megatron" come out.

2019

Cardi B's debut studio album *Invasion of Privacy* wins a Grammy for Best Rap Album.

CHAPTER 4

STARDOM

PINK FRIDAY

Nicki's debut album *Pink Friday* came out in late 2010. She thought the album would do well. Still, the singer was nervous. People told her it was hard to be successful as a woman who rapped.

The rapper didn't need to worry. Her record hit number one on the Billboard 200 list. It took less than three months. This was only the fourth time a female rapper had earned that spot. "I hope that this opens doors for all of the girls everywhere," she said to V-103 radio.

INVASION OF PRIVACY

Before releasing their first studio albums, both Nicki and Cardi B built up a following. This helped their music succeed quickly. *Invasion of Privacy* was Cardi B's first official album. It came out in 2018. All 13 songs on the album were gold certified. This means each one sold more than 500,000 copies. Cardi B was the first female artist to do this.

"SUPER BASS"

One of the most popular singles from *Pink Friday* was "Super Bass." It reached number three on the Hot 100 list. This was the second highest for a female rapper. Many people thought this was the song that truly made Nicki a hip-hop superstar. In 2011, it was the most streamed song in the U.S. The song's music video was the most watched of the year too. In it, Nicki performs as her character Barbie. She wears a pink dress and a large pink and blond wig.

"I LIKE IT"

"I Like It" was a huge success for Cardi B. The track is on *Invasion of Privacy*. It features rapper Bad Bunny and singer J Balvin. A song from 1967, "I Like It Like That," is sampled on the track. This means part of the melody is used. Hitting number one on the Hot 100 set another record for Cardi B. She was the first female rapper to have two songs make it to that position.

GUINNESS WORLD RECORDS

Guinness World Records has kept track of all kinds of records since 1955. Both Nicki and Cardi B have made it into the book. Nicki's record is for most Billboard Hot 100 entries by a solo artist (female). She reached it with 76 hit songs. Aretha Franklin had held the title before, with 73 tracks. In 2018, Cardi B set a record for most simultaneous Billboard U.S. Hot 100 entries by a female. This broke Beyoncé's record. It didn't hold for long, though. Billie Eilish broke Cardi B's record in April 2019.

STAR APPEARANCES

Soon Nicki had many big appearances. She performed as a special guest in the 2012 Super Bowl halftime show. The rapper M.I.A. and superstar Madonna sang with her. That same year, Nicki did a guest appearance on *American Idol*. Later, the show invited her to be a judge for its 12th season. The episodes aired in 2013. Many showed a feud between Nicki and Mariah Carey. Carey was also a judge.

BILLBOARD CHARTS

Billboard magazine started posting pop music charts in the 1940s. They showed which songs were the most popular each week.

There are many modern Billboard lists. Some follow all music. The main list is called the Hot 100. It shows the top 100 songs. Other lists are specific to a kind of music, like country, R&B, pop, or rock.

Rankings for songs and albums depend on how many times they are played on the radio. They also count social media. The number of copies sold is important too.

TV PERSONALITY

Success brought more appearances for Cardi B as well. To promote *Invasion of Privacy*, she cohosted *The Tonight Show*. The singer was on with regular host Jimmy Fallon.

In 2019, Netflix announced a new show called *Rhythm + Flow*. It is a hip-hop talent show. Cardi B was invited to be a judge. Chance the Rapper and T.I. are also judges. The show searches for new talent in different cities.

ON THE BIG SCREEN

Nicki began branching out from music. She voiced a character in the animated film *Ice Age: Continental Drift* in 2012. Two years later, Nicki had a big role in the film *The Other Woman* with Cameron Diaz. Then she appeared in *Barbershop: The Next Cut* in 2016.

In May 2018, *Saturday Night Live (SNL)* invited Nicki to be the musical guest. It was her third time as the main performer. She performed for the season finale.

Nicki with Leslie Mann, Cameron Diaz, and Kate Upton

Offset

"BE CAREFUL"

In April 2018, Cardi B was the musical guest on *SNL*. It was her first time on the show. The star performed "Bartier Cardi" and "Bodak Yellow." Later in the show, she sang "Be Careful." She appeared onstage in a white dress. Partway through the song, the camera moved back slowly to show viewers that the singer was pregnant. This was Cardi B's way of making an announcement. In 2017, she had married rapper Offset. The couple were expecting a baby in summer 2018. By 2019, the YouTube video of the song had more than 8 million views.

FAMILY MATTERS

Nicki moved out of her family's house when her younger brother was just a child. One day he asked when she would be back. "And it just broke my heart," Nicki told *The Fader*. The singer is close to her siblings, even though she doesn't see them very often. "I just miss them. Every time I talk about them, I get emotional," she added.

BECOMING A MOM

Cardi B gave birth to a baby girl on July 10, 2018. Her daughter is named Kulture Kiari Cephus. Her middle and last names come from Offset. His real name is Kiari Kendrell Cephus.

After the baby was born, Cardi B cancelled a tour with Bruno Mars. She wanted to spend more time with her daughter. "I respect mothers more than ever now. I see moms differently," she explained to *Vogue*.

MORE ALBUMS

Nicki stayed very busy. The rapper from Queens kept releasing more albums and singles. "Starships" from *Pink Friday: Roman Reloaded* was another big hit. This album made it to the top of the charts in 2012. The next year, she had songs on the Hot 100 list 44 times. In 2014, *The Pinkprint* came out. Nicki's hit song "Anaconda" was on this album. "You should . . . always be trying to show that you're the best," Nicki said to *Billboard* magazine.

TOP BILLBOARD HOT 100 SINGLES

● **NICKI MINAJ**

#3	Super Bass	4/2011
#5	Starships	2/2012
#2	Anaconda	8/2014
#10	Chun-Li	4/2018
#20	Megatron	6/2019

CONTINUED SUCCESS

Cardi B kept breaking records in 2019. *Invasion of Privacy* won a Grammy for Best Rap Album. It was the first time a solo female performer took home the award. The record also won Album of the Year at the BET Awards. The rapper from the Bronx had worked her way up to the top. "I feel like my life is a fairy tale and I'm a princess—rags to riches," she said about her success in *Harper's Bazaar.*

CARDI B

#1	🎵	**Bodak Yellow**	6/2017
#14	🎵	**Bartier Cardi**	12/2017
#1	🎵	**I Like It**	5/2018
#13	🎵	**Money**	10/2018

CHAPTER 5

INFLUENCES AND COLLABORATIONS

HIP-HOP AND POP

Nicki's earliest recordings were all hip-hop. As her fame grew, her music started to become more mainstream. She released more pop-style songs. At first, Nicki wasn't sure she wanted to go this direction. "I felt like my pop music made me have to retell my story," she noted to *The Fader.* Later, she focused again on hip-hop. Different styles helped her grow as an artist. "Looking back now, I love that I was pushed to reinvent myself," she added.

TWO PASSIONS

Like Nicki, Cardi B got her start with hip-hop music. However, some of her songs and albums have other styles. Latin music is one of her influences. Caribbean is another. This music was common in Washington Heights and the Bronx. The star has been honest about her musical style choices. She wants to release music that people will buy. "I have a passion for music, I love music. But I also have a passion for money and paying my bills," she said in an interview with *The Fader*. Both passions show up in her rapping.

Madonna

ALL ABOUT SHOUT-OUTS

Nicki prides herself on giving shout-outs to
people. "Nowadays, it's become cool to pretend
[you] weren't influenced by other artists," she said on
Instagram. She doesn't agree. Recognizing inspirations
is important. Some of her influences are Madonna and
Cyndi Lauper. Female rappers Foxy Brown, Lil' Kim,
Missy Elliott, and Trina also shaped Nicki's style.

LADIES FIRST

Like Nicki, Cardi B has also talked about being inspired by female rappers. One of the first albums she ever bought was by Missy Elliott. Khia and Trina have influenced her music. Two of Cardi B's favorites are Lady Gaga and Madonna. She has also pointed out how important Nicki's work has been in her career. "[She's] somebody I listened to ever since I was in high school," the rapper posted on Instagram.

EAST COAST VS. WEST COAST

East Coast rappers have a different style than those on the West Coast. East Coast rap tends to have faster tempos. The music is easy to dance to. West Coast rap is often more relaxed and slower.

In the 1990s, there was a feud between East and West Coast rappers. The main rivalry was between West Coast rapper Tupac Shakur and East Coast rapper Notorious B.I.G. They used their music to insult each other. Feuds still exist between rappers. However, the East Coast and West Coast rivalry has ended.

David Guetta

IMPORTANT COLLABORATIONS

Nicki's first big collaborations were with Lil Wayne.
Their three mixtapes were *Playtime Is Over*, *Sucka Free*,
and *Beam Me Up Scotty*. These helped start Nicki's career.
David Guetta is another artist she has worked with. He
is a French music producer and DJ. As of 2018, they had
worked on five songs together. Their 2015 song "Hey
Mama" made it to number eight on the Hot 100 list.

"LA MODELO"

An important collaboration for Cardi B was the song "La Modelo." The 2017 single was by the Puerto Rican artist Ozuna. He wanted her to sing on his track. But he didn't want her to rap. Ozuna told *Billboard* that Cardi B said, "I don't sing; I'm a rapper and not an artist." However, he managed to convince her otherwise. She recorded the vocals in Spanish and English. The song demonstrated her strong singing voice.

Ozuna

Ariana Grande

ALBUM GUEST STARS

Nicki's albums feature many guest stars. *Pink Friday: Roman Reloaded* was released in 2012. The album includes songs with Nas, Jeezy, and Bobby V, among others. More stars joined her on the 2014 album *The Pinkprint*. Ariana Grande and Meek Mill are featured on the album. Chris Brown, Lil Wayne, and Drake performed on both records. Beyoncé also sang with the rapper on "Feeling Myself." Just before that, Beyoncé had asked Nicki to star on her remix of "Flawless." Nicki talked to radio station Hot 97 about it. "I want you to be you. I don't want you to hold back," she said Beyoncé told her.

"FINESSE"

In 2017, Cardi B met Bruno Mars backstage after his concert. They decided to work on a song together. He invited her to record vocals for a remix of his track "Finesse." The two enjoyed the collaboration. "Don't let this crazy music business change who you are. . . You're a true star," he told her on Instagram. Cardi B's 2018 album featured many guest stars. One collaboration was with Migos on the song "Drip." Artists 21 Savage and Chance the Rapper were also on the album.

INVASION OF PRIVACY SHOUT-OUTS

Cardi B's album *Invasion of Privacy* includes many shout-outs to fellow artists. She especially calls out female singers. The rapper wanted to show her appreciation for other performers. For example, she mentions the group TLC. Also mentioned are singers Tina Turner and Rihanna. Beyoncé gets the most shout-outs. Her name is mentioned four times on the album.

FEATURED ARTIST

Many musicians have wanted to work with Nicki. She has been a featured artist on their tracks. In 2017, Nicki and Cardi B were featured on "MotorSport" with the rap group Migos. Nicki has rapped with several big stars. These include Mariah Carey, Usher, and Christina Aguilera. In 2019, she was a featured artist on songs by Megan Thee Stallion, Jason Derulo, and Post Malone, among others.

"GIRLS LIKE YOU"

"La Modelo" was just one song that featured Cardi B. Like Nicki, she has performed on tracks for other artists. Bruno Mars, Rita Ora, and Jennifer Lopez are just a few of the stars who have asked her to work with them. "Girls Like You" is a song Cardi B recorded with the group Maroon 5. The song was first released in 2017. A new version came out the next year. This one featured a rap verse from Cardi B. It eventually became a number-one hit.

SHARED INFLUENCES

Nicki and Cardi B were influenced by the female rappers who came before them. Here are a few of their inspirations.

Foxy Brown

- Rapper from Brooklyn, New York
- Sometimes called the "Female Tupac;" has been compared to Nas and Jay-Z
- First album: *Ill Na Na* (1996)
- Guest appearance on Nicki's track "Coco Chanel" in 2018

Lil' Kim

- Hip-hop artist from Brooklyn, New York
- Discovered in 1994 by rapper The Notorious B.I.G.
- In a feud with Nicki since 2007; has praised Cardi B

Missy Elliott

- Grew up in Virginia
- Formed an all-female R&B group called Fayze in 1989
- Congratulated Cardi B when "Bodak Yellow" came out

Trina

- Artist from Miami
- First album came out in 2000; sixth album released in 2019
- Album *Still Da Baddest* hit number six on Billboard 200

Eminem

QUEEN OF RAP

Nicki's fourth album, *Queen*, was released in 2018. She had collaborated on tracks with Eminem and The Weeknd. The next year, she performed with Ariana Grande at the Coachella festival.

The busy star had made a name for herself in a difficult industry. She explained her path to becoming the "Queen of Rap." "I work hard for what I have and if you want to be successful, you have to work hard," she said on the TV show *The View*.

BRONX DREAM COME TRUE

Cardi B also worked on more collaborations in 2019. "Please Me" with Bruno Mars was her second song with the singer. She is also featured in Ed Sheeran's song "South of the Border."

The regular girl from the Bronx had made it. All of her life experiences helped shape her into the star she is today. "Everything that's going on where I'm from, it really influenced me. It really influenced my music," she said in an interview with Music Choice.

Bruno Mars

CONNECTED LIVES

Female rappers haven't had an easy time making it in music. Nicki and Cardi B had to prove themselves in the music industry. Their lives in and around New York City weren't always easy. Still, they never gave up on their goals.

TAKE A LOOK INSIDE

ARIANA GRANDE

TWO EXTRAORDINARY PEOPLE.

CAMILA CABELLO

CHAPTER 1

EARLY LIFE

WHO IS ARIANA GRANDE?

Ariana Grande was born in June 1993. The singer's full name is Ariana Grande-Butera. Her family is of Italian American heritage. She is from Boca Raton, Florida. It is about an hour north of Miami. Ariana's name came from a character named Princess Oriana in *Felix the Cat: The Movie.*

WHO IS CAMILA CABELLO?

Camila Cabello is a good friend of Ariana. When she was born, her parents named her Karla Camila Cabello Estrabao. This was in March 1997. The pop star is of Cuban and Mexican heritage. Her birthplace is Cojimar, Cuba. As a child, she spent time in both Havana and Mexico City. When the future star was six, she moved to Florida. Her family still lives in Miami.

BRANCHING OUT

In 2011, Ariana took a risk too. People already knew her from *VICTORiOUS*. Still, she wanted to do more with music than a *VICTORiOUS* soundtrack. Acting was fun, "but music has always been first and foremost with me," she told *Rolling Stone*. Ariana had opened a YouTube account in 2007. Now she began uploading many songs. The risk was a success. Her covers of Rihanna, Mariah Carey, and others got over 10 million views. That was before she was even offered a record deal.

MORE FIFTH HARMONY

At first, Camila loved being in Fifth Harmony. "I was so excited that it wasn't over because I wanted to just keep going on that journey. . . . I was like a kid in a candy store," Camila told Lena Dunham in her podcast. However, she soon started feeling frustrated. There was not enough freedom. She did not want to keep singing songs someone else wrote.

PARALLEL LIVES

Born in Florida

Spoke English as her first language

Loved performing from a young age

Born in the 1990s

Sings in soprano voice

Has a sibling who is also into music and performing

Lived in South Florida

Born in Cuba

Spoke Spanish as her first language

Was shy as a child

GIVING BACK

Ariana gives back to causes she believes in. As a girl, she and her mother formed a theater group called Kids Who Care. The group sang at charity events. Later, the singer donated her money from concerts. One was for victims of violence at the 2017 white nationalist rally in Charlottesville, Virginia. Another was for Planned Parenthood. Both Camila and Ariana are vegans. They also care about the environment. The stars each used their social media platforms to spread awareness of the 2019 Amazon rain forest fires.

DOING HER PART

In 2016, Camila worked with Save the Children. She designed a "Love Only" T-shirt. Her important social media messages end with those words. The T-shirt was sold to raise money for girls' education and health care. Another group she has worked with is the Children's Health Fund. It provides health care to poor families. In 2017, the singer and Lin-Manuel Miranda released "Almost Like Praying." The song raised funds for the victims of Hurricane Maria in Puerto Rico.

TOP BILLBOARD HOT 100 SINGLES

● ARIANA GRANDE

#2	**Problem** featuring Iggy Azalea	6/2014
#3	**Bang Bang** featuring Nicki Minaj, Jessie J	10/2014
#1	**Thank U, Next**	11/2018
#1	**7 Rings**	2/2019
#2	**Break Up with Your Girlfriend, I'm Bored**	2/2019

● CAMILA CABELLO

#20	**I Know What You Did Last Summer** featuring Shawn Mendes	1/2016
#4	**Bad Things** featuring Machine Gun Kelly	2/2017
#1	**Havana** featuring Young Thug	1/2018
#6	**Never Be the Same**	5/2018
#1	**Señorita** featuring Shawn Mendes	8/2019

FOR MORE TITLES AND INFORMATION $\longrightarrow$

CONNECTED LIVES™